*What
We Know
about
Heaven*

WHAT WE KNOW ABOUT HEAVEN

JAMES A. NELSON

Tyndale House Publishers, Inc.
Wheaton, Illinois

All Scripture quotations are from *The Holy Bible,*
New International Version, copyright 1978 by New
York International Bible Society.

First printing, December 1986

Library of Congress Catalog Card Number 86-51167
ISBN 0-8423-7921-5
Copyright 1983 by James A. Nelson

*This book is dedicated
to Rita Lentz Moran,
whose confidence in God
when facing death
made heaven real
to all who knew her.*

CONTENTS

1 *Meet Rita*   11

2 *What Is
Heaven Like?*   17

3 *Who Is
in Heaven?*   45

4 *What Goes On
in Heaven?*   59

5 *What Are the
Living Conditions
in Heaven?*   71

6 *How to Enter
Heaven*   95

7 *Meet
Yourself*   107

PREFACE

It's ironic! The hope of heaven can become one of our most subtle adversaries on earth. What God intended to be a garland of fragrance and beauty around our necks may turn out to be a ball and chain fastened onto our ankles. This happens when we become so absorbed in thinking about heaven that we fail to get involved with life on earth and make the contribution to our times God intended we should. As the old saying goes, we may get "so heavenly minded we are no earthly good."

I pray this doesn't happen to you. Promise God and yourself that you will read about heaven not only looking forward to going there but also purposing that what you learn will make you a more useful person in this world.

ONE
Meet Rita

I stepped out of the home of Tom and Rita Moran one sunny November morning a few days before Thanksgiving. I was carrying a little green card file, like the one you probably have at your house holding three-by-five-inch recipe cards. I stood quietly for a moment before opening the car door and thought how that card file had in it something more precious than a solid brick of gold.

Rita had known for two months that she was dying, and cancer was the culprit. Her doctors had tried various treatments. The medicines and radiation had arrested the disease for awhile, but now it had asserted itself again and nothing could be done to halt its lethal course. Much prayer had gone up for Rita. But it evidently was not the will of our perfectly wise and totally loving heavenly Father to give her physical healing.

So Rita began an in-depth, thorough search of the Bible to discover what God says about heaven. After all, she was going there and would be arriving soon. It was only natural that she wanted to know what her destination was like. We do the same thing when we read pamphlets about a place we plan to visit on vacation. Only Rita was going to make heaven her permanent home. She wouldn't be coming back—that is, not until the Lord Jesus comes again. Then she and all other Christians who have died will accompany him.

She realized it was possible that some Scriptures on heaven might elude her quest. So she asked Christian friends at her church and elsewhere to send her their favorite Bible verses about heaven. Rita joined these quotations with what she had discovered, and she put them all together in her green card file. The result was as complete a collection of the words of God dealing with heaven as I have seen. That's why, to me, that card file held something more precious than gold.

Within hours Rita was to reenter the hospital and would probably not come back again to the lovely home she and Tom shared. She requested that I, her pastor, take these three-by-five-inch cards on which the Bible references were written and put them into a form that the Lord could use to help others. This book is my attempt to do so. In a real way this book is a joint project: Rita's and mine. It represents her last effort at serving the heavenly Father here on earth. Now she delights in her fellowship with him in his home.

So that you might breathe a little bit of the atmosphere of this adventure, perhaps you should hear directly from Rita. On October 23, 1981, she wrote:

This was to have been a Christmas letter, but of necessity it will also be a till-we-meet-again greeting. Since I am not sure how many good days are left for me (perhaps a month, the doctor says), I wanted to write now to express my Christmas wishes for you and to let you know how excitedly I am anticipating my first Christmas in heaven. . . .

It is not everyone who can be given sixty to ninety days' notice, and I am so very grateful to the Lord for this time. It has enabled me to do much for Tom and for Mother, my two greatest concerns. . . .

My time these days is spent writing out recipes for Tom, sorting and labeling items to be given away, initiating Tom into my bookkeeping systems, etc. My special delight, however, is a study I am doing on heaven—gathering all the facts I can from Scripture about the place, the personnel, their activities, the "living conditions," etc. It has been a great blessing and comfort to me, and I am hoping to have the results duplicated in some way so that others, too, may benefit. In case I am unable to finish the task, our pastor has enthusiastically offered to take over for me. . . .

Knowing that shortly I must put off this my tabernacle, even as our Lord Jesus Christ has shown me . . . I endeavor that you may be able, after my death, to have these things always in remembrance.
Love,
Rita

Let's open the little green card file and see what's in it. We just may be on the threshold of becoming very wealthy people. That is exactly what we will be if heaven is more to us than simply a word in the Bible. When heaven becomes a vivid reality for us, we can be fabulously rich in a possession that will never be lost or devalued. We become the owners of a hope that gives unimagined strength for life on earth and bright-eyed, eager anticipation for life in heaven.

TWO
What Is Heaven Like?

When facing the question, "What do we know
about heaven?" we would have to answer,
"Nothing. Nothing by personal, firsthand
experience through being there, that is."
People living in this age of information
explosion know many things their parents
and grandparents never thought of. But as far
as hands-on acquaintance with heaven goes,
there has been no advance in knowledge.

It takes a reliable and trustworthy individual who has been in heaven to tell us about it.
The best person we could find to meet this
requirement is our heavenly Father. Not only
is he in heaven; he owns it! The Bible is a
book in which, among other important things,
God tells us about heaven. He gives us a
personally conducted tour of his home where
he has lived forever.

Up the coast from where I live in California is a large, elaborate, breathtaking residence. It's called Hearst Castle. Millions of people have toured through it. Well-informed, congenial guides take visitors to various areas in the house. They do a good job of explaining the history of the castle, telling about the rare and beautiful treasures in room after room. But no one for the last few decades has been taken through by the master of the house, William Randolph Hearst. So a lot has been missed that only Mr. Hearst could share.

It's not that way with heaven. The Lord of that place gladly and personally talks about it. He tells us all we are able to comprehend—not everything, just what will be understandable and helpful for those of us who still live on earth. Listen to what is written in 1 Corinthians 2:9-10: "As it is written, 'No eye has seen, no ear has heard, no mind has conceived what God has prepared for those who love him'—but God has revealed it to us by his Spirit. The Spirit searches all things, even the deep things of God." Our holy Guide shares some wonderful general information about his home. He does so lovingly and selectively with the desire that we all join him to live there forever.

HEAVEN IS HOLY

The Bible refers to heaven as God's "holy dwelling place" (Deut. 26:15; 2 Chron. 30:27). John, in his apocalyptic vision, "saw the Holy City, the new Jerusalem, coming down out of heaven from God" (Rev. 21:2, 10). Nothing less than this could be expected since God in his very nature is holy and heaven is his home.

For a place to be holy means that it is perfectly pure and clean in every detail. Heaven, therefore, is a place that is absolutely good—a true utopia. In this it differs from any other environment human beings have ever known, because all people are corrupted by sin.

Since heaven is holy, total personal spiritual cleanness is the entrance requirement. "Nothing impure will ever enter it, nor will anyone who does what is shameful" (Rev. 21:27). God does not tolerate sin in his presence. We can't be where a holy God is without having acceptable holiness ourselves. "An impossibility!" you cry. You are right if you are thinking of human effort only. We are so unlike God that a drastic change is necessary and none of us can pull it off.

God himself is the only one who can make

us good enough to live in a holy heaven. He has accepted the challenge and made possible what is humanly impossible. Jesus Christ is God's answer. Christ died on the cross for the sins of the world, and all who personally trust this Savior are pure enough for heaven. As the Bible affirms, "The blood of Jesus, his Son, purifies us from all sin" (1 John 1:7). And "Christ loved the church and gave himself up for her to make her holy, cleansing her by the washing with water through the word, and to present her to himself as a radiant church, without stain or wrinkle or any other blemish, but holy and blameless" (Eph. 5:25-27).

HEAVEN IS REGAL

It is kingly. The seat of the government of the kingdom of God is there. It is an environment of incomparable majesty. The courts of Israel's King Solomon or of England's Queen Elizabeth can't compare with the royalty of heaven. Have you ever dreamed of living in a king's palace? Heaven is your place!

The throne of God is there. This was the first thing the Apostle John saw when he looked into heaven. The throne seemed to fill his vision. He witnesses, "I was in the Spirit, and there before me was a throne in heaven with someone sitting on it" (Rev. 4:2). All the teaching in the Bible about the sovereignty of God and the kingdom of God finds its culmination at the throne in heaven where God rules supreme forever.

In times when we wonder what this old world is coming to, it's reassuring to know that the loving, almighty God is governing. He is still in control of the universe. When you think about people in heaven, think about them being at the center of where the worldwide, significant action is. They realize intensely the royalty of the Lord with all the delight that brings.

Rita used to remark often that she wanted the Lord's way in her life. She fully believed that as Holy King he knows and desires the best for his people. Now she experiences how wise that conviction was. She's in the regal place. She sees the King.

HEAVEN CONTAINS WONDERFUL TREASURES
You've often gone into a home and been struck with certain outstanding furnishings. Maybe an oriental rug. Or a fascinating painting. Or a beautiful lamp. Heaven is a

place where certain special contents catch the eye and rivet the attention.

In heaven there is a sort of divine library. Only two books are mentioned by the Bible as being in this "library." One is the Book of Life in which the name of every believer in Jesus is written (see Exod. 32:33; Luke 10:20; and Heb. 12:22-23). "Only those whose names are written in the Lamb's book of life" will be permitted to enter heaven (Rev. 21:27). This book is the official register of the citizens of heaven. Philippians 4:3 mentions believers "whose names are in the book of life." It must be quite a thrill to see one's name in that great book!—and a big reason to express love to Christ, who made it possible for our names to be inscribed on its pages.

The other massive volume in heaven contains the complete record of the deeds of all people. Every person. Every act. In the day of God's judging of human beings, reference can be made to the accurate record in heaven. All complaints will be referred to this book.

Then I saw a great white throne and him who was seated on it. Earth and sky fled from his presence, and there was no place for them. And I saw the dead, great and small, standing before the throne, and books were opened. Another book was opened, which is the book of life. The dead were judged according to what they had done as recorded in the books. The sea gave up the dead that were in it, and death and Hades gave up the dead that were in them, and each person was judged according to what he had done. Then death and Hades were thrown into the lake of fire. The lake of fire is the second death. If anyone's name was not found written in the book of life, he was thrown into the lake of fire. Revelation 20:11-15

Not too many years ago this concept of the books in heaven might have seemed incredible. Not any more! We've got computers down here on earth that can do just about the same thing. And these computers are being improved all the time. Thousands of pieces of information fit on a silicon chip the size of your little fingernail! God's records in heaven don't seem so impossible after all. And of course, God has the power and ability to do anything he wants.

Another treasure in heaven is the ark of the covenant. "God's temple in heaven was opened, and within his temple was seen the ark of his covenant" (Rev. 11:19). This is not

the one Moses had made by Israel's crafts-
men, but the original, of which Moses' ark
was a copy. This item serves as a focal point
of God's presence among his people. God is
present and always available to those who
enter his home in his way. A believing person's
presence in heaven is all because God is
trustworthy; all his words are true.

One of the most awe-inspiring scenes in
heaven is the Holy City, the new Jerusalem,
prepared by the Lord and awaiting the moment when it descends from heaven to take
its unique role in God's plans.

> Then I saw a new heaven and a new earth,
> for the first heaven and the first earth had
> passed away, and there was no longer any
> sea. I saw the Holy City, the new Jerusalem,
> coming down out of heaven from God,
> prepared as a bride beautifully dressed for
> her husband. And I heard a loud voice
> from the throne saying, "Now the dwelling
> of God is with men, and he will live with
> them. They will be his people, and God
> himself will be with them and be their
> God." Revelation 21:1-3

The Holy City is an indescribable city of gold,
diamonds, pearls, and precious stones, with

an exquisite beauty such as no one has ever seen. The Holy City is 1,500 miles in length, breadth, and height—about the distance between Los Angeles and Kansas City. After the first heaven and the first earth have passed away, this city will be a part of the recreated earth and is the place where believers will live with God for eternity. Also, his city represents the Bride of Christ, God's people, the Church.

HEAVEN IS GLORY

Asaph, one of King David's choirmasters, was the writer of Psalm 73. In this psalm he speaks in part about heaven. Having asked why people who don't love God have it so good when he had it so rotten, Asaph finds that his final answer rests with God:

> I am always with you;
>> you hold me by my right hand.
> You guide me with your counsel,
>> and afterward you will take me into glory.
> Whom have I in heaven but you?
>> And being with you, I desire nothing on
>> earth.
> My flesh and my heart may fail,
>> but God is the strength of my heart
>> and my portion forever.

The key phrase about heaven is "You will take me into glory." Heaven is called "glory"—a clear statement of fact. As Asaph points out, nothing is quite so rich as knowing God is always with his people in any circumstance of life. The Lord's presence continues through life and death and into heaven, which Asaph calls glory. The two words are synonymous. What a heritage belongs to the child of God!

Since glory holds such a key place in defining heaven, what is glory? In the Old Testament, glory spoke of value and honor. It was an epithet for kings. When a Greek word was sought in the New Testament to render this concept of glory accurately, one was chosen that speaks of stunning radiance, great brilliance. Heaven is put forward as a place of awe and dazzling beauty unequaled by anything made by God or man. The result is exuberant, indescribable joy for the persons who are there.

Glory also characterizes the children of God who are in heaven. Here's how the Bible states this marvelous truth: "I consider that our present sufferings are not worth comparing with the glory that will be revealed in us" (Rom. 8:18). The thought appears again in 2 Corinthians 4:17-18: "For our light and momentary troubles are achieving for us an eternal glory that far outweighs them all. So we fix our eyes not on what is seen, but on what is unseen. For what is seen is temporary, but what is unseen is eternal." This is an excitingly personal feature to grasp. Not only are God and the place glorious, but so are the persons who once were so imperfect and un-glorious on earth. As you try to imagine what your godly loved ones and friends are like in heaven right now, think of them as not only being in glory but possessing glory.

Every child of God in heaven is a real heavyweight, carrying around a weight of glory, like that of God, that will last forever. As far as the heavenly Father is concerned, every individual trusting Christ but still walking around on this earth is as good as already in this wonderful place. Paul noted, "Those he justified, he also glorified" (Rom. 8:30). In brief, this conclusion is unavoidable: the soul trusting in Christ continues forever in a place called "glory" and in a matching condition that is also called "glory."

HEAVEN IS HOME
A location holding one of the warmest places in our hearts and experiences is home. Buried deep in the soul of most people is a

special warm feeling for that place. It seems that human beings have been created to enjoy the blessings of a home. So the composer writes, "Be it ever so humble there's no place like home," and Bing Crosby sings, "I'll be home for Christmas." We can identify with the sentiment. People spend millions of dollars each year to fly or drive many miles to get home, even for a couple of days. God has provided heaven as the supreme satisfaction of this homing instinct. Heaven is a home where God lives and where his family, death-experience by death-experience, is joining him.

One of the most familiar verses in the Bible states the fact this way: "In my Father's house are many rooms. . . . I am going there to prepare a place for you" (John 14:2). You probably live in a home on a certain street at a certain number. People can write to you there, phone you there, visit you there. God also has a home address where he may be contacted: heaven.

The Apostle John isn't the only one who gives information about where God lives. Isaiah implores God, "Look down from heaven and see from your lofty throne, holy and glorious" (Isa. 63:15). Stephen in his moving speech to the Jewish Sanhedrin said,

"The Most High does not live in houses made by men. . . . 'Heaven is my throne, and the earth is my footstool' " (Acts 7:48-49). In King Solomon's prayer dedicating the beautiful temple he had built, the king spoke no less than seven times of God living in heaven (see 1 Kings 8:22-53).

So it is not childish fancy to think of heaven as the place where God is at home. It's a reality, a clear fact. Granted, he is present here on earth, for there isn't a place we can escape from God and hide. He is everywhere. This is true, yet in a special way God lives in heaven. Our minds may have trouble reconciling these two facts, but that doesn't change their reality. So we will believe the truth that in his total being God is at the same time everywhere generally and in heaven specifically.

With legitimate excitement we decide that heaven is not only the place where God lives but the dwelling place for every follower of Jesus Christ, where he or she can live and feel at home. When God's children leave this life and go home, they immediately begin an experience of God's grace, care, and love such as they've never known. The thoughtful efforts of both Father and Son have combined to provide living places for all God's children in this heaven. The provision is in keeping with his perfect, divine awareness of each and every Christian. He knows what will bring perfect fulfillment to an individual's soul, what will totally bless that unique person.

"My Father's house," as Jesus called it, is big enough to receive all God's people, millions upon millions of them. No need to worry about overcrowding or running out of space. Everyone will be satisfied with the provision. So when you say about Christians who have died, "They've gone home," you're absolutely right, more accurate than you can imagine. Consider what a magnificent thing it must be for them to catch the first glimpse of the dwelling place the Lord lovingly made just for them.

The changeless purpose of this divine revelation is clear. Jesus says, "Let not your heart be troubled" (John 14:1). Heaven is likened to a home so that all anxious fear and uncertainty about what happens to a child of God after death can be banished. There's not a thing to worry about! How this renews our faith in the heavenly Father and the Lord Jesus. Don't miss the urgency of Christ's words, "Believe in God! Believe also in me!" We need faith in the Lord.

To trust God for a home in heaven brings

one courage in life, especially as death draws near. Shortly before he died, noted scientist and staunch Christian, Dr. Harry Rimmer, wrote to Dr. Charles E. Fuller of the "Old Fashioned Revival Hour." Note the anticipation, courage, and confidence Dr. Rimmer displayed:

Next Sunday you are to talk about heaven. I am interested in that land, because I have held a clear title to a bit of property there for more than fifty-five years. I did not buy it. It was given to me "without money and without price." But the donor purchased it for me at a tremendous sacrifice. I am not holding it for speculation, since the title is not transferable. It is not a vacant lot.

For more than half a century I have been sending materials out of which the Great Architect and Builder of the Universe has been building a home for me, a home which will never be remodeled or repaired, because it will suit me perfectly, individually, and will never grow old. Termites can never undermine its foundations, for they rest upon the Rock of Ages. Fire cannot destroy it. Floods cannot wash it away. No locks or bolts will ever be placed on its doors, for no vicious person can ever enter that land where my dwelling stands, now almost completed and almost ready for me to enter in and abide in peace eternally, without fear of being rejected.

I hope to hear your sermon on heaven next Sunday from my home in Los Angeles, but I have no assurance that I shall be able to do so. My ticket to heaven has no date marked for the journey, no return coupon, and no permit for baggage. Yes, I am all ready to go, and I may not be here while you are talking next Sunday—but I shall meet you Over There someday.

HEAVEN IS PARADISE

It is not unusual for everybody to use words at one time or another that they don't fully understand. Like little children listening to adults, we often pick up terms and repeat them without realizing what we're saying. *Paradise* may be one of these.

The Bible thoughtfully and rightfully calls heaven "paradise." People living in the time the Bible was written would understand better than we what the word *paradise* signified. We want to grasp the concept as they did, understanding in a meaningful way this characterization of heaven.

Today's Iran was yesterday's Persia, the Persia where fabulously wealthy monarchs ruled. Their palaces were spectacularly and unimaginably rich and beautiful. Surrounding and penetrating the palaces of the Persian kings were beautiful parklike gardens, immaculately kept. Often these gardens were walled so that the beauty could be enjoyed exclusively by the ruler, his family, and the royal court. At other times the king provided beautiful gardens for the enjoyment of the public, maybe as a bid for their loyalty. In the Middle Iranian language, each exquisite royal garden was called a paradise.

It's not surprising, then, that *paradise* was used by the man on the street in Bible times to speak of a place of supreme beauty and enjoyment. Usually he thought of it as being located above the earth. The Bible appropriates this word as a name for heaven with all these implications.

Jesus used *paradise* in speaking to the repentant, believing thief dying next to him. "I tell you the truth, today you will be with me in paradise" (Luke 23:43). Christ was on his way to heaven—paradise—and he promised to take the trusting robber with him there before the day was done. The man had pled, "Jesus, remember me when you come into your kingdom" (v. 42). Jesus identified the kingdom as paradise.

Another example of *paradise* as a name for heaven can be read in 2 Corinthians 12:1-4. This is a brief, firsthand report of an amazing experience in Paul's life. In telling of the incident, Paul says he "was caught up to paradise" (v. 4). Paul calls this paradise where he went "the third heaven" (v. 2). We wish Paul had said a whole lot more about paradise, but it seems that the magnificence of what he saw outdistanced the use of words to describe it. He called it "paradise" but gave no further description. It must have been a glorious experience, because God even gave him a physical problem to keep him from becoming conceited (v. 7).

Often dying Christians on their way to heaven have said rapturously, "Oh, it's so beautiful over there!" The exclamation is valid, for that's what heaven is really like. As no place else, heaven is paradise! And believers such as Rita who have left this life are now there, hearing, seeing, and experiencing realities and beauties that can't be put into words.

HEAVEN IS REST

Resting brings a number of common thoughts to mind. It's what you do after a period of hard work or strenuous exercise. You rest when you stretch out on the bed or push back in your reclining chair. Sometimes rest is emotional relief, such as when you say your mind is at rest about a certain problem and you've stopped worrying about it. When we go to sleep we rest. Our physical and mental batteries are recharged. But even all of these concepts put together are not quite what the Bible means when *rest* is used to define heaven.

Hebrews 4:9-11 is the part of the Bible dealing with heaven defined as rest. "There remains, then, a Sabbath-rest for the people of God; for anyone who enters God's rest also rests from his own work, just as God did from his. Let us, therefore, make every effort to enter that rest, so that no one will fall by following their example of disobedience." The context of this section draws a parallel between Israel's Promised Land and the heaven into which God the Father brings his children. As Canaan was a place called "rest," so heaven is a place called "rest"—only heaven is perfect in this quality. Both Canaan and heaven are highly desirable. Yet many Israelites missed Canaan rest, and we may miss heaven rest. God doesn't want us to lose out, but we might if we don't follow his way and trust his Son, our Lord and Savior Jesus Christ.

Two words used in Hebrews 4:9-11 are both rendered "rest" in English. In verses 10 and 11 a term is employed that carries the idea of a place where one settles down and lives, active in the events going on. Heaven has this quality of rest for those who live there. It's a place where meaningful things are happening. By "rest" the Bible does not mean heaven is filled with people lying around in heavenly hammocks, swinging and yawning their way through eternity. *Rest* is used as it relates to our heavenly Father when he asks, "What is the place of my rest?" (Acts 7:49). We know he isn't lounging away in heaven but is busy about everlasting matters.

The second word for rest in Hebrews 4:9-11 is very special. It is found in verse 9 and can be described as a Sabbath-type rest, a rest such as God experienced after the six days of creation. It is this kind of rest the inhabitants of heaven experience. By this special word we know that living in heaven is marked by a sense of achievement, enjoyment, and satisfaction. Can you feel the proper emotion of Sabbath-rest in the sentence, "God saw all that he had made, and it was very good" (Gen. 1:31)? This is God reveling in the fruit of his labor. People in heaven are enjoying this same kind of delight. They have satisfaction and enjoyment. God is saying, as it were, "Heaven is a place where I share with my people my state of mind, my emotional life, how I have felt since the time I created all things."

It logically follows that Sabbath-rest is not unconsciousness or sleep. God didn't take a nap on that seventh day! On the contrary, Sabbath-rest is living in possession of all personal faculties functioning at peak performance. You can't imagine God in heaven as only partially operative, and you shouldn't think of the inhabitants of heaven as being that way either. Sabbath-rest means they're wide awake. There is a complete aliveness, every faculty at its zenith.

Sabbath-rest also carries the sense of the fulfillment of a previous occupation and a continuing involvement with it. What a person does in this life has a result that continues in heaven. Life on earth and life in heaven have a serious relationship. What you do now to the Lord's glory has everlasting consequences. You've just begun to enjoy the fruits of your Christian efforts. Don't give up the good work!

What you do in everyday life is significant if you dedicate your job to the Lord. It's a part of you that will never be lost. What you are and do for him here are joined to what you will be and do in heaven, the Sabbath-rest. "Blessed are the dead who die in the Lord from now on . . . they will rest from their labor, for their deeds will follow them" (Rev. 14:13). This is a great challenge to live for God, enter into ministry, and serve the Lord. Your works will follow you into eternity. This is what Sabbath-rest is!

Maybe this is part of what Jesus meant when he urged us all to lay up treasures in heaven. Listen to these words and relate them to your life today: "His master replied, 'Well done, good and faithful servant! You have been faithful with a few things; I will put you in charge of many things. Come and share your master's happiness!' " (Matt. 25:21).

It is not too much to say that the rest of heart that comes at the time one accepts Jesus into his life as Savior and Lord is a bit of the quality of heaven coming to us now, though its fullness will be reached only when

heaven is entered. This alone is reason
enough for welcoming Christ into our human
experience.

So precious is heaven as rest that a clear
statement is made in the Bible as to how to
gain it. "Let us, therefore, make every effort
to enter that rest, so that none will fall by
following their example of disobedience"
(Heb. 4:11). Nothing is more worthy of a
person's diligent concern than securing this
rest God has promised. God asks earnest and
genuine faith in Christ, obedience to his way.
The consequences of disobedience because
of unbelief are fatal, keeping you from heaven
entirely. Make it a point to enter into heaven-
rest now.

HEAVEN IS A BETTER COUNTRY
Nationalism is a strong force in our world.
Personal pride in one's native land has moti-
vated millions of individuals to march off to
war. National pride has always been an
important factor in world diplomacy. Even
today the fierce hatred between the Israelis
and the Palestinians has its roots in a burning
spirit of nationalism on the part of both these
peoples. There is something special about
each country on the face of the earth, and it is

proper that citizens of every nation should express their loyalty and patriotism.

But the best country you could imagine can't begin to measure up to heaven. Note what Hebrews 11:13-16 has to say:

> All these people were still living by faith when they died. They did not receive the things promised; they only saw them and welcomed them from a distance. And they admitted that they were aliens and strangers on earth. People who say such things show that they are looking for a country of their own. If they had been thinking of the country they had left, they would have had opportunity to return. Instead, they were longing for a better country—a heavenly one. Therefore God is not ashamed to be called their God, for he has prepared a city for them.

The note of superiority is clear. Heaven is a "better country." That's the way God evaluates it.

When God created people, he gave them the ability to live in both the earthly and the heavenly world. Every person has a soul, a distinct personality by which he relates to other people. Personhood is expressed through a physical body that speaks and acts, a body made specifically for an earthly environment. It breathes earth's air and is sustained by earth's produce. This soul-and-body person lives in a certain country on the earth.

God also put a spirit in people. It can't be seen, but it is just as much a part of a person as a hand or foot. This spirit is the part of a human being where God and man meet. God designed it especially to live in the heavenly environment—a heavenly country, as Hebrews puts it. But Paul distinguishes between a natural body and a spiritual body (see 1 Cor. 15:44), so when a person goes to heaven, his spirit still indwells a body, one that is made to last forever.

Both the earthly country and the heavenly country are real, one as real as the other. But the heavenly country is eternal, whereas the earthly country is for the years of one's physical life only. God will never force a person into the heavenly country. Each of us must choose to go there by welcoming Christ into our life as Savior and Lord.

The author of Hebrews uses two words in speaking of the supreme country. In verse 14 the word *country* is not used strictly in the sense of territory, a few square miles of land.

Rather, *country* has the thought of a nation, a fatherland, where one's family is, the place of one's ethnic group.

So heaven is the place where one has a perfect sense of belonging because he has trusted Jesus and is a member of God's family. It is the place of gathering for people of the same spiritual nationality. Presently the child of God is staying for awhile on planet earth, but he's a pilgrim passing through, only temporarily in the earthly country. The place where he will settle down eternally is heaven. He's headed for the supreme country. Paul wrote, "Our citizenship is in heaven. And we eagerly await a Savior from there, the Lord Jesus Christ" (Phil. 3:20).

The second word used in Hebrews 11 to tell of the supreme country is *city* (vv. 10, 16). This speaks of a spirit of community on a national level, a community of congenial people experiencing eternal togetherness. Here everything is organized as in a well-run city, and there is a sense of righteousness and peace. It's like the delight of feeling, "I'm back where I belong."

The author of Hebrews mentions the patriarchs: Abraham, Isaac, and Jacob. From these men, who did have abundant life on earth, we learn that earthly things can never fulfill a human being. One's looking and longing must be forward and upward. The realities of permanence and settledness can be found only in the supreme country—as Abraham, Isaac, and Jacob discovered. Looking forward to the supreme country regulates life here in our earthly land. This honors and pleases God and makes him glad to say we are his people. He is constantly available to us and not reluctant to say to all the listening angels, "I am their God."

THREE
Who Is in Heaven?

Heaven should never be thought of as a beautiful but silent and unoccupied mansion. It is not some cold, black hole in the sky. In various ways God tells us heaven is a place where persons actively live, each exercising the full range of his or her unique personality. Heaven has an identifiable population. And a large, diversified group it is!

The first thing to be understood about people in heaven is that the essentials of what it means to be a person don't change when a person goes to heaven. All the basics of personhood are still fully possessed. The only difference would be that these features are enjoyed to perfection.

The elements in personhood are three:

intellect, emotion, and will. Every person in heaven has an intellect capable of the finest reasoning, including thinking about oneself. Heaven's blessings become very personal, keen, and fulfilling because of this. How often the exclamation must arise from God's children in heaven, "Look at what I am and the wonderful experiences coming my way!"

Being a person, every individual in heaven has emotion, such as love, on the highest level. The person able fully and purely to love and receive love discovers what it really is to be a person. Since the population of heaven has emotion, it is possible there will be a degree of sadness, too, particularly because of the absence of someone whom the person would very much like to have there with him. However, heaven's sublime joy will override any level of disappointment. It does for Christ, and so it must be for God's children.

People in heaven also have wills. They are able to make voluntary decisions based on the data to which heaven has exposed them. Decisions about things to do in heaven, courses of action to take, the best and most rewarding ways to be involved in heaven's scene. A feeling of achievement because of wise decisions is part of being a person in heaven.

Without a doubt, people there are complete persons. We're not dealing with something we can't put our hands on or understand. Nor are we talking about half-persons or quarter-persons or any fraction of being a person. Heaven is populated with full persons.

Look more carefully at who these persons are. Don't think of them as a mass, but single them out in groups or as individuals. Think of people such as Rita who thought and studied so much about heaven. Or perhaps you know someone in heaven who is very special and dear to your heart—husband, wife, parent, child. Each of them is absolutely and vibrantly alive.

THE TRINITY

God the Father, God the Son, and God the Holy Spirit are in heaven. That's rather obvious, but it deserves a little further thought. The particular emphasis of the Bible is on the presence in heaven of God the Father and Jesus Christ who is God the Son. Perhaps the Holy Spirit is little mentioned since he lives uniquely in the lives of God's children now.

It is comforting to be able to affirm that God the Father is in heaven. That's why the Bible so often speaks of him as the heavenly

47

Father. The emphasis placed upon his person is not that of monarch or judge, though he is both. The stress rather is upon his capacity of father in the total perfection of that concept. God is not a flawed father as most earthly fathers are. He is a perfect father acting in perfect wisdom and fullest love. In this character he will forever express himself. This is how he is acting right now toward all who are in heaven.

A conviction like this ought to bring warmth and strength to all who properly pray, "Our Father in heaven, hallowed be your name" (Matt. 6:9). The encouragement coming from God's fatherhood should be powerful as those who trust in Christ hear the Savior say, "I am returning to my Father and your Father, to my God and your God" (John 20:17). Heaven is not only a place, it is a state of living in the full enjoyment of what it means to have God as one's Father. The relationship begun on earth through the new birth, by faith in Jesus Christ, is continued perfectly in heaven.

The Lord Jesus Christ is also there. He clearly stated this when he said, "I came from the Father and entered the world; now I am leaving the world and going back to the Father" (John 16:28). The Apostle Peter is among others who record that Jesus Christ "has gone into heaven and is at God's right hand—with angels, authorities and powers in submission to him" (1 Pet. 3:22; see also Col. 3:1). It is not too much to say that Jesus is the central person in heaven's population.

Hebrews 9:24 declares, "For Christ did not enter a man-made sanctuary that was only a copy of the true one; he entered heaven itself, now to appear for us in God's presence." You have to wonder: how does Jesus appear in heaven? What qualities do those who are there see in him? Rita, and many others like her, who loved Christ and served him, now see him as he truly is. But what do they especially appreciate about the Lord Jesus?

The symbolism of Revelation 5:6 can help to answer these questions. John records, "Then I saw a Lamb, looking as if it had been slain, standing in the center of the throne, encircled by the four living creatures and the elders. He had seven horns and seven eyes, which are the seven spirits of God sent out into all the earth." This is what children of God in heaven are seeing in Jesus and appreciating about him. He is the almighty Savior who gave his life for the world. He is a magnificent combination of might, majesty, and meekness. What he was on earth he still is in heaven. The Lamb is the symbol of the kingdom of heaven. Not America's eagle, England's lion, France's tiger, or Russia's bear. Jesus as the Lamb of God is the embodiment of the grace of God and is forever appreciated as such in heaven.

Here'a a truth that must not be missed! Jesus is in heaven as the almighty Savior, the resurrected God-man who lived on earth. That's how he is seen. The population of heaven identifies him that way. He's there with a risen, glorified human body as heavenly proof of the fact that all God's children shall one day have perfect bodies like his. Paul puts the matter this way, "Christ has indeed been risen from the dead, the firstfruits of those who have fallen asleep" (1 Cor. 15:20).

OBEDIENT ANGELS

The Bible distinguishes between obedient angels and disobedient angels and describes the activity and future of both groups. Our concern in this book on heaven is centered on the obedient angels only. (As for the disobedient angels, let Jude 6 suffice: "The angels who did not keep their positions of authority but abandoned their own home—these he has kept in darkness, bound with everlasting chains for judgment on the great Day.")

The obedient angels belong to heaven. It is their home in a special way. Jesus spoke of them in Matthew 24:36 as "the angels in heaven." Similar emphasis can be seen in Matthew 18:10: "See that you do not look down on one of these little ones. For I tell you that their angels in heaven always see the face of my Father in heaven." Jesus knew, because he had lived in heaven surrounded by these obedient angels more thousands of years than one can imagine.

One of the exciting things about being in heaven is to see the angels. They play quite a part in God's plans. The story of the angels is not confined to one book, one writer, or one period in Scripture. Angels are mentioned 273 times in thirty-four books of the Bible.

Angels seem to be organized as a group. Their special association is an ordered unity consisting of thrones, powers, rulers, and authorities (see Col. 1:16; Eph. 3:10). This would indicate that angels are occupied with many enterprises. These persons in heaven have spheres of service and degrees of position. Two angels high in the angelic hierarchy are Gabriel and Michael (see Luke 1:19 and Jude 9).

Though not as mighty as God, angels in

heaven are powerful personages. In Revelation 5:2, an angel is described as "mighty." David emphasizes this when he says, "Praise the Lord, you his angels, you mighty ones who do his bidding, who obey his word" (Psa. 103:20). Clearly, strength is a characteristic of angels, but so is volition, or will; some angels are obedient and some are disobedient.

Adding to this awe at seeing the obedient angels is their vast number. They are count-less, an innumerable army. John, who saw this massive group, reports in Revelation 5:11, "Then I looked and heard the voice of many angels, numbering thousands upon thousands, and ten thousand times ten thousand." And every one of these grand creatures moves very swiftly. Isaiah describes it as flying (Isa. 6:2).

It goes without saying the angels of heaven are busy. The citizens of heaven watch them as they go about following Christ's orders. Peter says Christ has "angels, authorities and powers in submission to him" (1 Pet. 3:22). One of these tasks the angels perform for Christ is to serve some of the needs of people on earth who are God's children. Speaking of the angels, the author of Hebrews asks rhetorically: "Are not all angels ministering spirits sent to serve those who will inherit salvation?" (Heb. 1:14).

In an old church in Scotland these words are inscribed, "Though God's power be sufithink to governe us, yet for man's infirmitie he apointeth his angels to watch over us." That's old English to us, but the truth of the words is up-to-date and encouraging.

In everything they do, angels are one of the most effective groups in declaring the glory, majesty, might, and holiness of God in heaven. And believers in the Lord like Rita watch all this activity! Can you imagine the eagerness with which they do so? They have never seen anything like this in all their lives! No one in heaven or on earth should worship angels, but everyone ought to highly regard them. One thing is sure: God's children will appreciate the obedient angels forever.

FOLLOWERS OF GOD FROM OLD TESTAMENT DAYS

Enjoying heaven is not just for godly people who have died since the advent of Christ. Persons from way before that time are in heaven, people like Abel, Noah, Abraham, Joseph, Isaiah, Daniel, and thousands of folks less well known than these men. In Hebrews 12:23 they are called "the spirits of righteous men made perfect." The term "spirits" signifies persons who have been freed from the limitations of a human body. They are in heaven and are no less real people than when they lived on earth. These are persons of pre-Christian days who trusted the Lord's revelation to them in their particular age. They just came to God believing what he said and followed his way.

A small delegation from this group in heaven once came to earth in Jesus' lifetime. There were only two of them, and it was a dazzling experience. Matthew tells it this way: "After six days Jesus took with him Peter, James and John the brother of James, and led them up a high mountain by themselves. There he was transfigured before them. His face shone like the sun, and his clothes became as white as the light. Just then there appeared before them Moses and Elijah, talking with Jesus" (Matt. 17:1-3). Peter's excited words in the next verse show that these two Old Testament figures, though now heavenly beings, are recognized and appreciated.

Can you imagine Rita in heaven meeting some of these historic persons? Maybe listening to them tell of their walk with God in their time? Or asking them things she often wondered about? This could well be the case. Heaven brings all good things to perfection, so fellowship there between the children of God is closer than we have ever imagined. Heaven provides and promotes a unity and friendship that spans all of earth's history.

THE CHURCH OF JESUS CHRIST

Jesus came into the world to give people an opportunity to become children of God, to put them into a worldwide fellowship called the Church, the body of Christ, and to take each of them to be with him after they die. God's children comprise a great family of people with special benefits because of their position. One of these bestowed benefits is to live in heaven with the heavenly Father after their time on earth is over.

The Bible states the matter this way: "You have come to Mount Zion, to the heavenly Jerusalem, the city of the living God. You have come to thousands upon thousands of angels in joyful assembly, to the church of the firstborn, whose names are written in heaven." (Heb. 12:22-23). The words *joyful assembly* give special insight about the children of God in heaven. The words are intended to speak of a festival gathering. They paint a picture of great joy, even exuberance. The church in heaven lives in a most happy atmosphere. This reality of the church in heaven so overwhelmed Paul that he declared, "I kneel before the Father, from whom his whole family in heaven and on earth derives its name" (Eph. 3:14-15).

That part of the family of God now in heaven is just as much multinational as the segment of the family still on earth. They have a song that praises Christ. It goes in part, "You were slain, and with your blood you purchased men for God from every tribe and language and people and nation" (Rev. 5:9). There may be a common heavenly language in which the family of God sings this song, but national distinctions still are noted. Jesus' mission touches people from all over the world. In heaven there is a mixture and variety of nationalities with the freshness this brings. There is no dull sameness, though all share equally in the Lord's saving act.

Another quality is noted about the church in heaven. It is a triumphant group. "I looked and there before me was a great multitude that no one could count, from every nation, tribe, people and language, standing in front of the Lamb. They were wearing white robes and were holding palm branches in their hands" (Rev. 7:9). Though this part of the family arrives in heaven out of a deeply troubled experience, it reflects the whole group. Palm fronds cut and waved were, in Bible days, symbols of victory and great joy. They were used this way on the first Palm Sunday when Jesus rode into Jerusalem as the victorious Son of David coming in the name of the Lord (see John 12:12-13). There's no feeling of defeat on the part of the church in heaven. They have a sense of victory that is eternal. No wonder there is joy unbounded there.

An aged Christian whose name is unknown once wrote something that makes you think about God's family in heaven. It is entitled simply, "Heaven":

When I was a boy I used to think of heaven as a glorious golden city with jeweled walls and gates of pearl, with nobody in it but the angels, and they were all strangers to me. But after awhile my little brother died. Then I thought of heaven as that great city, full of angels, with just one little fellow in it that I was acquainted with. He was the only one I knew there at that time.

Then another brother died, and there were two in heaven that I knew. Then my acquaintances began to die, and the number of my friends in heaven grew larger all the time. But it was not till one of my own little ones was taken that I really began to feel that I had a personal interest in heaven. Then a second went, and a third, and a fourth.

So many of my friends and loved ones have now gone there, that it seems as if I know more in heaven than I know on earth. And now, when my thoughts turn to heaven, it is not the gold and the jewels and the pearls that I think of — but the loved ones there. It is not the place so much as the company that makes heaven seem beautiful to me.

FOUR
What Goes On in Heaven?

Most parents can identify with the following experience, especially if their children are teenagers. You plan what you think is a nice trip for the family, maybe to some outstanding national park like Yellowstone or the Grand Canyon. And the first thing the children say after you've told them about it is, "What's there to do in Yellowstone Park or the Grand Canyon?" Right then the wind goes out of your sails and you feel like parking the kids with Grandma while you take the trip alone.

Something similar to this reaction may be true as one thinks about heaven. You may never tell anyone because you think they may consider you terribly unspiritual or ungrateful. But you wonder to yourself, "What does a person do in heaven, anyway?" Frankly the Bible doesn't fill us in on this to the extent we might like. Probably God is saving some wonderful surprises for his children when they come home to heaven to live.

But we can identify two broad activities. In heaven the children of the Lord are engaged in pursuits that can be classified as (1) observation and (2) occupation. These happy people are both spectators of the heavenly scene and participants in it.

OBSERVATION

That people in heaven can observe and evaluate suggests the possession and use of personal faculties with which one has been familiar every day on earth. In heaven there is a continuity of what it has been to be a person living in any earthly city or hamlet. Only, in heaven these human faculties are at their finest. They convey their impressions and messages fully. The story of the rich man and Lazarus, the beggar, found in Luke 16:19-31, portrays these two men in their life after death as still being human—thinking, talking, desiring as they did on earth.

Though the things observed in heaven are

wider and more numerous than we can tell, the Bible talks about a few of them. Children of God in heaven see Christ clearly in his glory. Jesus incorporated this fact in one of his prayers: "Father, I want those you have given me to be with me where I am, and to see my glory, the glory you have given me because you loved me before the foundation of the world" (John 17:24). Notice the almost indescribable splendor in John's revelation of Jesus Christ:

I saw seven golden lampstands, and among the lampstands was someone "like a son of man," dressed in a robe reaching down to his feet and with a golden sash around his chest. His head and hair were white like wool, as white as snow, and his eyes were like blazing fire. His feet were like bronze glowing in a furnace, and his voice was like the sound of rushing waters. In his right hand he held seven stars, and out of his mouth came a sharp double-edged sword. His face was like the sun shining in all its brilliance.

When I saw him, I fell at his feet as though dead. Then he placed his right hand on me and said: "Do not be afraid. I

am the First and the Last. I am the Living
One; I was dead, and behold I am alive for
ever and ever!" Revelation 1:12-18

This must be one of heaven's most breathtaking and soul-stretching experiences, to look
on Christ in his exalted and honored state.
What a contrast to his earthly humiliation!

Of course, to engage in this observation
requires a transformation of us human
beings. The glory is too blinding for earthly
eyes. But Christ takes care of that when we
trust him as Savior and are born again. As
Jesus prayed, "Father, the time has come.
Glorify your Son, that your Son may glorify
you. For you granted him authority over all
people that he might give eternal life to all
those you have given him" (John 17:1-2). Rita
and others in heaven, seeing Christ in his
glory, must be saying something like, "It was
worth it to trust in and follow Jesus of
Nazareth, even in the valley of pain."

In heaven God's child also observes his
heavenly Father. And, we might add, quite
intimately. David had this outlook and wrote,
"In righteousness I will see your face; when I
awake, I will be satisfied with seeing your
likeness" (Psa. 17:15). Seeing God's face and
his likeness will be all a person could ever

ask for! Jesus gave a promise about this experience, too. "Blessed are the pure in heart," he said, "for they will see God" (Matt. 5:8). And Jesus knew what a wonderful event that would be. He had seen the heavenly Father face-to-face for eternity.

Rita had a serene, sweet face. Her face expressed what was in her heart. It's that way with all of us. The face has a way of showing what's deep inside us. So to see God's face is to observe how deeply he loves us. How totally he accepts his children and welcomes them to heaven! What a depth of satisfaction that brings to heaven's population. They don't see a frown or a scowl but God's smiling face. What it has been to know him here is but a small part of what it is to see his face there.

God the Father is observed in action also, particularly in special ministries to each of his children. The Bible says, "God raised us up with Christ and seated us with him in the heavenly realms in Christ Jesus, in order that in the coming ages he might show the incomparable riches of his grace, expressed in his kindness to us in Christ Jesus" (Eph. 2:6-7). What an amazing sight! God is actively engaged in doing kind and gracious things for his own in heaven—the warmest, most loving, most personally-suited things that ever happened to a person—and all in a measure surpassing our ability to calculate.

God's grace is an eternal blessing. All this begins the moment a person steps into heaven, and it never ends. Rita has been experiencing this personal touch from God for many months now. You may have seen the most spectactular sights this life on earth has to offer. But none of them can begin to match what people in heaven are seeing.

OCCUPATION

People in heaven not only look at the sights, but they participate in meaningful activity. Heaven is not an eternity of idleness. Nor is it tiring, routine busyness. On the contrary, heaven is worthwhile, fulfilling involvement. Heaven fairly hums with activity—and all of it top-flight!

People in heaven actively worship the Lord. Revelation 4:1-11 shows us the throne of the Lord in heaven. Notice especially verses 4 and 10: "Surrounding the throne were twenty-four other thrones, and seated on them were twenty-four elders. They were dressed in white and had crowns of gold on their heads. . . . The twenty-four elders fall down before him who sits on the throne, and worship him who lives for ever and ever. They lay their crowns before the throne." These elders represent all the children of God since Adam. Their white robes speak of the forgiveness and righteousness God has given them. Their crowns represent the victories they experienced in living for God. That victory has reached its peak by their presence in heaven.

This worship is not the lifeless and possibly dull activity many people think worship is. Worship is the highest duty and privilege of man. It is the chief activity for which human beings have been created. Worship is the first and fundamental claim of God upon his children. Jesus said, "God is spirit, and his worshipers must worship in spirit and in truth" (John 4:24).

Worship is the directing of deepest emotions toward a worthy, soul-satisfying object. That object alone can be the Lord. Worshiping him is the highest release of one's most profound impulse. It is pure adoration, a great outflow of love, a commitment of self to the Person of supreme worth. The children of God worshiping him in heaven achieve their highest potential for which God created them.

The reward for the worshiper is supreme delight; it is his finest accomplishment in heaven. This activity is not one long, endless church service but is the happiest experience anyone could ever have. In the final analysis, worship of God is what being a person is all about.

Nine times out of ten, worship is accompanied by music. (This can be true even in your daily life if you whistle and worship as you go about your daily tasks.) In heaven the music is singing. It's an expression of the joy a person feels there. It is giving voice to gratitude and, as such, is not sad or gloomy as is so much singing on earth. The thankfulness of the song has to do with what Jesus achieved upon his cross for everyone.

> They sang a new song: "You are worthy to take the scroll and to open its seals, because you were slain, and with your blood you purchased men for God from every tribe and language and people and nation. You have made them to be a kingdom and priests to serve our God, and they will reign on the earth." Revelation 5:9-10

This singing is pure praise to God. There is nothing in it of self-praise. Everything is happy praise to Christ. The song the Apostle John quotes may have been composed just for this great occasion of being in heaven. Undoubtedly it is only one of a number of songs of a similar nature. This is real singing! It honors Jesus Christ the Savior and brings another dimension of joy to God's children. How beautiful it must be!

"How Great Thou Art!" is an old hymn that is sung often these days. The last verse fits perfectly with thoughts of worship in heaven:

When Christ shall come with shouts of
    acclamation
To take me home, what joy will fill my
    heart!
Then I shall bow in humble adoration,
And there proclaim, my God, how great
    Thou art!

Rita joined many times with our congregation to sing this hymn. This song, and others with a similar theme, will continually be sung to God in exuberant worship.

There is another occupation in heaven. It arises naturally from worship. Generally stated, this occupation is serving God. It is useful, worthwhile, God-honoring activity. Revelation 22:1-4 describes the heavenly city with its River of Life and Tree of Life. Let one phrase in verse 3 catch your attention: "His servants will serve him." God's own in heaven are at the same time sons, daughters, and servants of the Lord. This differs little from what they are on earth. It's just that the ministries are performed in a different place.

Everyone in heaven serves the Savior. Following God's direction, each person serves in his own way, as do the angels with their assignments. But for no one is this service burdensome toil. It is a privilege with rich blessing. The children of God serve him by means of the abilities and gifts bestowed on them by the Holy Spirit when they were on earth. The abilities cultivated here continue to function there. This life is preparation for activity in heaven's life. For this reason it is so wise to know our gifts from the Lord now and to exercise them diligently. Each child of God has at least one of these gifts and abilities, and these do not stop with death. Jesus has planned for your gift to be used in heaven's eternity.

Rita was a wonderful servant of the Lord on earth. She was a missionary, a college registrar, and a teacher—a competent organizer who precisely carried out what she organized. Rita fulfilled these roles on earth very well and to the Lord's glory. She and her talents are still at work in the service of the same Master.

There is one more occupation in heaven. It's a little different from worship and service. We could call this occupation "Operation Eternal Friendship." It is the activity of personal, individual fellowship with Jesus. Revelation 3:4 suggests this occupation: "They will walk with me, dressed in white, for they are worthy." The occupation of walking with Jesus is a continuance of the friendship established with him by faith on earth. As 1 John 1:3 tells us, "Our fellowship is with the Father and with his Son, Jesus Christ." In heaven this is a face-to-face activity, Jesus sharing with the person and the person with him. God's child not only participates in Christ's glory but also in the enjoyment of personal fellowship with him.

Through Operation Eternal Friendship, we take up the walk with God that Adam forfeited in the Garden of Eden (see Gen. 3). What the Lord has always desired he now is able to fulfill in heaven—meaningful, uninterrupted companionship with his children on a person-to-person basis. And these children of God reap an everlasting personal harvest of joy because of it. Centuries ago Enoch walked with God. So did Abraham. Now, so does Rita. And so shall we!

FIVE
What Are the Living Conditions in Heaven?

We all have had friends or relatives who have moved away. Perhaps they've gone to live in a famous city or an exotic country or in a rural setting. It's natural to ask them, "What is it like to live there?" Since heaven is a place, too, this same question arises in our minds as we think about that heavenly land. Our answer comes in a number of interesting observations from the Bible.

LIVING MUCH BETTER THAN HERE
In Chapter Two it was pointed out that heaven is a superior country. It naturally follows that living conditions there are better than the most pleasing situation on earth. Hebrews 11:16, speaking of people like Noah and

Abraham, remarks, "They were longing for a better country—a heavenly one." They wanted a better place to call home, a better set of living conditions. They knew they were strangers on earth. Most of us are at least somewhat sensitive to this deep inner yearning. These better conditions are found only in heaven.

Paul the apostle wrote about the desire for a fuller life. He noted, "Meanwhile we groan, longing to be clothed with our heavenly dwelling" (2 Cor. 5:2). On earth we live in a state of restriction. The potential for life is narrowed, limited by the bodies in which we are housed. Even the best body is imperfect, so living has its frustrations and sighing. This is not necessarily because of pain, but because we can't quite reach the full life we know should be ours.

In heaven this limitation is removed. The child of God is no longer weighed down and held back. His person is at its peak. Life is lived in fullness and intensity because it is free from the drawback of sin in thought, desire, or act. To live in heaven is to live the good life. Consider the plain statement of Philippians 1:23: "I am torn between the two:

I desire to depart and be with Christ, which is better by far."

The Apostle Paul made this point in another way when writing about how he personally felt: "For to me, to live is Christ and to die is gain" (Phil. 1:21). Something is gained by being in heaven. We have something in heaven we didn't have on earth. Living there goes beyond what it is to live on earth. Not only is Christ there, and that is gain, but something of advantage to the person is given. What has been done for the Lord on earth receives its reward. That reward can't be matched by what might have been experienced before heaven. Whatever the reward is, it is a genuine possession given the child of God, a worthwhile belonging. Hebrews 10:34 urges us to anticipate heaven's better life by reminding us that there we have "better and lasting possessions."

LIVING IN A SPIRITUAL BODY
When a child of God enters heaven, the moment after he leaves earth, he is given a spiritual body. It is a form in which to live. This form is perfectly suited to the environment of heaven and yet it retains the full

personality of the individual. The biblical basis for a valid expectation of this sort is 2 Corinthians 5:1-2: "We know that if the earthly tent we live in is destroyed, we have a building from God, an eternal house in heaven, not built by human hands. Meanwhile we groan, longing to be clothed with our heavenly dwelling."

The earthly, physical body is a temporary structure as it now stands. It is vulnerable to daily wear and tear. It is like a tent flapping and ripping in the hard winds of earthly life. Hippocrates, the father of medical science, viewed the human body just that way: "We don't live very long until we say, 'I can't do what I used to.' " Nobody can dispute this analysis. Paul, who wrote 2 Corinthians, had a growing consciousness of his failing physical faculties. For him, like all of us made in the image of God, this deteriorating and temporary condition of the body was hard to tolerate. That is why Paul encouraged believers about the spiritual body in heaven where earthly conditions cannot adversely affect it.

We ought to be clear, however, about our anticipated spiritual body. For instance, this body is something with substance. Heaven is not a place of disembodied spirits floating around in ghostlike form. People in heaven have real bodies—solid, identifiable, and well-built—in contrast to the tattered tents in which they once lived. This body is superior to the best body on earth. It is a special product of God's design and workmanship. No human hands play any part in either its construction or maintenance. The spiritual body is "eternal," suited exactly for the heavenly realms, so that heaven can be thoroughly appreciated and enjoyed forever without concern that the body will grow old and wear out.

You may honestly be wondering, "Is there some personal assurance for me that this spiritual body will be mine when I step into heaven?" Such a question is valid and under-standable, especially if your body is presently riddled with pain—as was Rita's. The affirma-tive answer is, "Yes, the Holy Spirit who lives in each child of God is our heavenly Father's promise to you." That assurance is stated by God this way, "It is God who has made us for this very purpose and has given us the Spirit as a deposit, guaranteeing what is to come" (2 Cor. 5:5).

Heaven is not peace that comes from extinction. It is not a departure into nothing-ness, nor is it even an absorption into deity. Rather, it is a place where God gives his child a spiritual body that is just as real as the physical body he received from his parents. In this spiritual body he lives to worship and serve God in heaven with meaningfulness and completeness. Now for Rita and all God's children in heaven the limited and often pain-dominated earthly body is gone. A new day and a new body have arrived! This is the vivid and glorious answer to Job's dismal and limited observation: "Man dies and is laid low; he breathes his last and is no more" (Job 14:10).

Let's conclude this discussion of the new body with Paul's glorious teaching in 1 Corinthians 15:40-57:

There are also heavenly bodies and there are earthly bodies; but the splendor of the heavenly bodies is one kind, and the splendor of the earthly bodies is another. The sun has one kind of splendor, the moon another and the stars another; and star differs from star in splendor.

So will it be with the resurrection of the dead. The body that is sown is perishable, it is raised imperishable; it is sown in dishonor, it is raised in glory; it is sown in weakness, it is raised in power; it is sown a natural body, it is raised a spiritual body.

If there is a natural body, there is also a

spiritual body. So it is written: "The first man Adam became a living being"; the last Adam, a life-giving spirit. The spiritual did not come first, but the natural, and after that the spiritual. The first man was of the dust of the earth, the second man from heaven. As was the earthly man, so are those who are of the earth; and as is the man from heaven, so also are those who are of heaven. And just as we have borne the likeness of the earthly man, so shall we bear the likeness of the man from heaven.

I declare to you, brothers, that flesh and blood cannot inherit the kingdom of God, nor does the perishable inherit the imperishable. Listen, I tell you a mystery: We will not all sleep, but we will all be changed—in a flash, in the twinkling of an eye, at the last trumpet. For the trumpet will sound, the dead will be raised imperishable, and we will be changed. For the perishable must clothe itself with the imperishable, and the mortal with immortality. When the perishable has been clothed with the imperishable, and the mortal with immortality, then the saying that is written will come true: "Death has been swallowed up in victory."

Where, O death, is your victory?
 Where, O death, is your sting?

The sting of death is sin, and the power of sin is the law. But thanks be to God! He gives us the victory through our Lord Jesus Christ.

LIVING IN FULL CONSCIOUSNESS
Believers in Christ do not enter unconsciousness when they die. Though *sleep* is sometimes used by the Bible in speaking of death, it describes the appearance of the body, not the state of the person who lived in that body. In heaven there is sharp consciousness with the full range of intellectual abilities. People there are aware, wide awake!

The story of the rich man and Lazarus, the beggar, in Luke 16:19-28 is one occasion in the teaching of Jesus Christ when he draws back the curtain and permits us to look at life beyond this present life. In this story, people die, but afterward they still have the ability to talk about things, to communicate with words. The dimensions of mental power still present after death are identical to those possessed before. Meaningful interpersonal relationships are built chiefly upon verbal communication. Jesus' teaching shows that this takes place in heaven between the persons living there. This relationship building includes Jesus Christ. To die is to go to be with Christ, not merely to look at him but to talk with him, too.

This full consciousness in heaven also includes the power to reflect, reason, and evaluate. Abraham asks the rich man to do just that, and he does so. He almost debates with Abraham! This reasoning ability is demonstrated in Revelation 6:10 where a group in heaven ask Christ with a loud voice, "How long, Sovereign Lord, holy and true, until you judge the inhabitants of the earth and avenge our blood?"

All of these alive intellectual abilities have to do with the practical nature of how life is being lived in heaven. Life goes happily on with minds working and thoughts communicated with words. Man, the social being who must communicate with fellow humans, does so on the highest and most rewarding level in heaven.

LIVING WITH FULL KNOWLEDGE

When I was a little boy in elementary school, I learned 1 Corinthians 13 during Daily

Vacation Bible School. I have never forgotten this chapter of God's Word. Along with millions of other Christians I have been inspired and challenged by what it says. It makes me look closely at the kind of Christian life I'm living. I appreciate the time the teacher took to help me memorize this great chapter about God's definition of love.

In developing the subject of love, God has Paul write about the time in history "when perfection comes, [and] the imperfect disappears" (1 Cor. 13:10). This perfect time has to do with being in heaven. When the day of entering heaven arrives, something happens for every child of God. "Now we see but a poor reflection; then we shall see face to face. Now I know in part; then I shall know fully, even as I am fully known" (v. 12).

In heaven we gain an ability to completely assimilate knowledge, to learn all there is to know in God's universe. We will be able to spend all eternity learning all the intricacies of life that God has always known. Paul puts forward a very bold and challenging parallel saying, "I shall know fully, even as I am fully known" (v. 12). As God knows me I shall have the ability to learn and know. That's learning at its fullest. What the mind cannot comprehend and absorb now it will be able to embrace in heaven. This chapter shows a progression in knowing: as a child, as an adult, and as a perfected person in heaven.

The city of Corinth in New Testament days was noted, among other things, for its manufacture of mirrors. They were made of highly polished metal. They were pretty good, but nothing compared to today's mirrors. The image the Corinthian mirrors reflected was imperfect at best. God is saying, "This is what earthly knowledge is—imperfect, incomplete, distorted." There is a degree of obscurity even in knowledge at its best. There are so many things we just don't know or know only fractionally. This is true even of one's present knowledge of Christ. In heaven incompleteness and imperfection of knowledge will give way to real knowing.

The child of God will have insights into the experiences he had on earth, insights he never had before. The unsolved puzzles of that life will be put together and God's loving purposes seen in everything. Unanswered questions about why things happened as they did will be answered. Finally the follower of Christ the Lord will understand. He will fully know about that life gone by, and he will love God for his wisdom. Divine providence on the personal level will become very clear in heaven. Until then God's children are to have absolute faith in the heavenly Father's wisdom and love.

This ability to excel in knowledge in heaven will bring immense satisfaction to every individual there. Created to learn and develop in knowledge, people will enter that experience with absolute ability to handle it. This will be another building block in the sense of security the person has as he lives in heaven. We now have a tendency to fear the unknown. Then there will no such thing as an unknown reality.

It is exciting to see how heaven fulfills the total personhood of a child of God. This happens physically, emotionally, mentally, spiritually, and socially. No part of the human being is left out. The whole person is rescued and restored to God's original intention in creation.

LIFE WITHOUT OPPRESSIVE, EARTHLY CIRCUMSTANCES

There are experiences in life we all could do without. They are intrusions into our happiness. They drag us down and keep us from vigorous living. They make getting through this earthly experience most difficult. In fact, these experiences may be more than some of us can bear, and sometimes suicide is the result.

It is otherwise in heaven. All those factors that together make up the volume of human misery are absent from that place. It was not the intention of God that these adverse elements ever be a part of human life. Man's sin introduced and perpetuated them. In God's home where his children are there is no place for adverse factors.

The Bible specifically identifies those oppressive aspects of earthly life that will be absent from heaven. There is no poverty in heaven. "Never again will they hunger; never again will they thirst" (Rev. 7:16). One of the heaviest burdens carried by the human family on earth is that of homelessness, poverty, and hunger. Thousands die each year at the hand of famine and exposure. In heaven all necessities are met abundantly.

The vicious trio with which we have to live on earth—suffering, death, and sorrow—is shut out of heaven. God says about heaven, "He will wipe every tear from their eyes. There will be no more death or mourning or crying or pain, for the old order of things has passed away" (Rev. 21:4). Rita longed to be free from pain. Her doctors used every skill they possessed to fight it. She was very brave by the strength of the Lord. Now all her suffering is gone. There is no such thing in heaven for any child of God. What a glorious release this is! Even though some of us still wrestle with pain on earth, we rejoice with Rita's painless experience now. And we look forward to sharing the same when we enter heaven.

A new law reigns in God's home. It is the opposite from that which permeates the earthly human family. The Lord told Adam and Eve that if they sinned they would die. They sinned and they died. Mankind has grappled with death ever since and has shed an ocean of tears. Most everyone somewhere during the course of living has confronted death. Henry Wadsworth Longfellow, in his poem "Resignation," observed:

There is no flock, however watched and
    tended,
But one dead lamb is there!
There is no fireside, howso'er defended
But has one vacant chair.

But the law of death can't be found in heaven; it has nothing to do with that place. It has no power there. Living is under a new law in heaven. That law is life, death's opposite. Paul writes of this new law that finds its fullness in heaven: "Through Christ Jesus the law of the Spirit of life set me free from the law of sin and death" (Rom. 8:2).

Because these oppressive circumstances are gone, it's little wonder there is complete joy in heaven. The emotional reaction of sorrow and crying never occurs. There is nothing in heaven to take away or diminish true, eternal joy. Long before Jesus was born David had this assurance and wrote about it, "You will fill me with joy in your presence, with eternal pleasures at your right hand" (Psa. 16:11). If living conditions are like this in heaven, a person would be a fool not to want to be there.

LIFE WITHOUT MARRIAGE

What is your deep-down feeling when told there is no marriage relationship in heaven? As a husband or wife, do you breathe a sigh of relief and say to yourself, "It can't come too soon as far as I'm concerned"? (If this is your reaction, you should seriously consider Christian marriage counseling.) Or does the knowledge of a marriageless heaven cast a bit of a cloud over your anticipation of going there? You've had a happy, satisfying marriage and can't imagine heaven without the re- lationship. (That sort of feeling speaks well for your marriage; share your secret with the miserably married!)

No matter what your response to the truth that life in heaven is lived without marriage, this is what Jesus says: "The people of this age marry and are given in marriage. But those who are considered worthy of taking part in that age and in the resurrection from the dead will neither marry nor be given in marriage" (Luke 20:34-35). Matthew 22:30 states: "At the resurrection people will neither marry nor be given in marriage; they will be like the angels in heaven." This is clear: no one lives in heaven in a marriage relationship with the wife or husband he or she had on earth. Marriage simply is not a part of heaven.

Not only does this observation touch most people with personal regret, it appears to be contrary to the fact that marriage is the original and highest form of human fellow- ship. It seems as though it should go on in the place of perfect fellowship. What's more, if marriage is a picture of the relationship between Christ and the Church, what could be more fitting than to have it continue as an eternal, visible expression of Jesus' oneness with and love for those who trust him?

Nevertheless, the statement of Christ is obvious. There is no marriage in heaven. Listening to the rebuke he gave the Sadducees in Matthew 22:29 ("You are in error because you do not know the Scriptures or the power of God"), we learn two things. The Bible never implies or teaches marriage in heaven. And knowing God's power, we believe he will replace the earthly marriage relationship with a better, heavenly relationship. Evidently marriage as we know it is not needed for optimum joy and fulfillment in heaven.

There is at least one problem that a heaven without marriage does away with. It is the difficulty that would arise if this weren't so for many of God's children who, while living on earth, have been married more than once. Thank God for the confusion that has been avoided for thousands of God's people who have scripturally remarried.

Knowing the heart of God and his plan for our highest good in heaven we conclude that in his home there must be a newer, finer relationship between those who have been married in this life. Certainly it will be nothing less than the best they have known. In heaven there will be no estrangement or lack of interest in each other, no obliviousness, no mere passing nods. Rather, the years put into earthly marriage will result in a relationship in heaven of deep, personal enrichment. The "much better" character of heaven applies to this feature as it does to all others. The prevailing patterns of life on earth are not the living conditions in heaven. We are not to think of heaven solely in terms of earth, nor eternity in terms of time.

LIVING MATURELY

Each child of God in heaven is consciously complete in every detail of his person. Finally everything in his being has come together and is whole. The goal for which he was brought into being has been reached. From this point on he is able to live completely. As a Christian he has reached adulthood, maturity, full growth in personality. The Bible states this fact twice. Paul writes of the time "when perfection comes" (1 Cor. 13:10). Hebrews speaks of people in heaven as "righteous men made perfect" (Heb. 12:23). In both cases, reference is made to what it is like to live in heaven. Each person lives maturely, with his or her essential being developed to perfection.

To live like this is the capstone of God's

desire and purpose for people. His goal has always been to have mature spiritual children. Now in heaven he has them. Personal maturity is the general quality of all who join the heavenly Father in his home. Paul declares this to be an objective of his Christian service: to "present everyone perfect in Christ" (Col. 1:28).

Maturity in heaven involves every aspect of personhood. The person's spiritual being, the deepest part of his nature, now can respond properly and fully in worship of God. Also, the body, the emotions, and the distinctive personality are perfected—in their highest quality. Undesirable features are dropped off like dead leaves. They have no place in heaven. You are your best self forever. You and everyone else will appreciate that!

Such absolute maturity doesn't exclude the effective use of your unique abilities. All those things that have prevented their full blooming are gone. Maturity takes over with all the satisfaction this brings. You're a smoothly running person in every part. What a high delight it is to be part of a population made mature. Imagine all the personality collisions that are avoided and the wonderful harmony in which people in heaven live!

In heaven God's people have been brought

to a point where the life and activities there can be fully appreciated. God's purposes for Christians in this life have been brought to a close and his purposes for them in heaven have begun. A truly significant goal has been reached. The day of death is the day of graduation—a true commencement. It is what living on earth has been all about. Now any deficiencies in personal development, in whatever area, have been made up.

What about little children when they die? Do they remain babies or small tykes forever? In light of life in heaven being lived maturely, this cannot be. Little children who die go to heaven but do not remain little children. The whole potential God built into them that was cut short by death is brought to completeness. They, too, are mature people in God's house. Age differences as we know them have no bearing. Maturity is the standard of measurement.

ENJOYING A HEAVENLY INHERITANCE
Usually part of being in a family involves, at some time or other, receiving an inheritance—that is, if there is anything to inherit. Something of value is freely passed along because of a special relationship and love.

The inheritance may be much or little according to the size of the estate. Children of God are people who have expectation for a great inheritance. The Bible elaborates upon this truth. "Praise be to the God and Father of our Lord Jesus Christ! In his great mercy he has given us new birth into a living hope through the resurrection of Jesus Christ from the dead, and into an inheritance that can never perish, spoil or fade—kept in heaven for you, who through faith are shielded by God's power until the coming of the salvation that is ready to be revealed in the last time" (1 Pet. 1:3-5).

Late in his life, Paul shared the intimate experience he had with Jesus on the road to Damascus. Christ is quoted as giving Paul a reason for becoming a Christian and preaching the gospel to others. "I am sending you to open their eyes and turn them from darkness to light, and from the power of Satan to God, so that they may receive forgiveness of sins and a place among those who are sanctified by faith in me" (Acts 26:17-18). Jesus is saying that this "place"—an inheritance—is part of being God's child. Having a right to this inheritance begins when a person is born into God's family by trusting Christ the Savior. Paul wrote, "You are no longer a slave, but a son; and since you are a son, God has made you also an heir" (Gal. 4:7). With a similar emphasis he said, "The Spirit himself testifies with our spirit that we are God's children. Now if we are children, then we are heirs— heirs of God and co-heirs with Christ, if indeed we share in his sufferings in order that we may also share in his glory" (Rom. 8:16-17).

Children of the Lord begin to dip into their inheritance now, in this life, by confidently claiming the many promises of God to Christians. But the bulk of the inheritance awaits arrival in heaven. Paul makes special mention of the fact that enjoying the inheritance to the full relates to being willing to suffer with Christ. This is having an unflinching faithfulness to him in the face of suffering. So often in the final days of her life Rita would honestly say through her pain, "I'm trusting the Lord; he knows what he is doing." This suffering with Christ in the lives of so many Christians does not call into question their being children of God. To the contrary, it is a pledge of inheriting with Jesus.

Life lived in heaven is in entering into the inheritance fully. It is not just possessing a title to the inheritance; it is realizing it completely. The inheritance enjoyed in heaven will not become polluted or wear out. It cannot deteriorate or be exhausted, and it is without defect. Only God's children can receive it.

While details of the inheritance are not given in the Bible, we know that it involves eternal life and perfect fellowship with God. As joint heirs with Jesus Christ, we will enjoy all that he possesses in heaven, including the unimaginable glory that will be his when history has reached its fulfillment. We will enjoy the new heaven and the new earth with Jesus. That's staggering! But as Jesus promised the Apostle John, "He who overcomes will inherit all this, and I will be his God and he will be my son" (Rev. 21:7).

SIX
How to Enter Heaven

This could just possibly be the most important chapter in this book. It is one thing to admire and desire a beautiful place. It is another to know the sure route to take you there—and then to get started on that route.

Much of the book you are reading is being written in the majestic Oak Creek-Sedona region of Arizona. The sights of towering cliffs and giant red-rock formations are indescribable. The sounds of the wind moving in the tops of the pines and the energetic creek rushing to join the Verde River are at the same time stimulating and relaxing. The pine needles form a soft blanket for the forest floor, and their scent refreshes the clear, sweet air.

Having just read this description of this beautiful place, you may really want to spend some time here yourself. But until you ask, "How do I get to Oak Creek-Sedona?" you'll never experience these sights, sounds, and scents. The same is true of heaven. Asking how to get there is the most serious and sensible inquiry you will ever make.

GOD'S REQUIREMENTS

God does have the right to establish requirements for coming into his home. After all, he owns it, and it is only by his grace that anyone ever joins him there. If we accept the right of a proprietor to put on the door of his business, "No bare feet, please," how much more we should extend to God the same right concerning heaven.

The heavenly Father requires that a person be clean from his sins before he can enter heaven. David asks and answers a serious question in this regard. "Who may ascend the hill of the Lord? Who may stand in his holy place? He who has clean hands and a pure heart, who does not lift up his soul to an idol or swear by what is false" (Psa. 24:3-4). There you have it! No one enters God's home still caked and contaminated with unforgiven sin.

Jesus, the Lord of heaven, further clarifies the matter of entering there. "Not everyone who says to me, 'Lord, Lord,' will enter the kingdom of heaven, but only he who does the will of my Father who is in heaven" (Matt. 7:21). As Jesus views the broad sweep of God's kingdom on earth and in heaven, he declares the necessity of earnest belief in Christ demonstrated by a life-style in keeping with God's will. One cannot toy with the reality of heaven if he is to enter it. Once the entrance requirements are known, action in keeping with them must be taken.

HOW TO MEET GOD'S REQUIREMENTS
The Bible is God's book. Its message makes the way of entering heaven unmistakably clear. As Rita drew near to the end of her earthly life, she felt very keenly that people must see and understand this divine way. She thoroughly searched out the Scriptures used in this book for that reason. The best hours of her last days were invested in this pursuit. It was a very wise investment. Nothing could be more important than knowing God's route to his home. No discovery made by any person in any period of history is more crucial.

The foundational fact of everything the

Bible says about entering heaven is that God himself makes provisions for that entrance. If he hadn't no one could ever get in. Isaiah recognized this. He had been given a glimpse into the awesome courts of heaven. He saw the Lord, high and exalted, with angels worshiping him (see Isa. 6:1). The prophet wrote, "I, even I, am the Lord, and apart from me there is no savior. . . . I, even I, am he who blots out your transgressions, for my own sake, and remembers your sins no more" (Isa. 43:11, 25).

In the New Testament, the heavenly Father's involvement in getting people into heaven is stated this way: "For God so loved the world that he gave his one and only Son, that whoever believes in him shall not perish but have eternal life. For God did not send his Son into the world to condemn the world, but to save the world through him" (John 3:16-17). "And we have seen and testify that the Father has sent his Son to be the Savior of the world" (1 John 4:14). The least that can be said is that God has gone all-out to make it possible for people to enter heaven. How generous! How gracious! How loving!

There is a changeless, eternal fact from which the truth about heaven comes. That fact is: "God is love" (1 John 4:8). If there were no loving God, there would be no heaven. However, the opposite is true. God does love us, and because of this we can anticipate heaven. The mighty rivers of our land have their sources high in the mountains. From these sources they rush in mighty climax to the oceans. So it is with heaven. Our hope of eternal life begins in the mountain of God's love. Gathering momentum it courses through our earthly experiences, culminating in heaven itself.

Paul expressed this idea as he wrote about God and his plan: "For he chose us in him before the creation of the world to be holy and blameless in his sight. In love he predestined us to be adopted as his sons through Jesus Christ, in accordance with his pleasure and will—to the praise of his glorious grace, which he has freely given us in the One he loves. . . . And he made known to us the mystery of his will according to his good pleasure, which he purposed in Christ, to be put into effect when the times will have reached their fulfillment—to bring all things in heaven and on earth together under one head, even Christ" (Eph. 1:4-5, 9-10).

Early in his ministry Jesus indicated the way to heaven is singular and uncompromising. Entrance is by one route only. There aren't a number of roads that end up in the same place. "Enter through the narrow gate. For wide is the gate and broad is the road that leads to destruction, and many enter through it. But small is the gate and narrow the road that leads to life, and only a few find it" (Matt. 7:13-14).

There are two gates and the right gate must be chosen. There are two roads and only one of them terminates in heaven. There are two groups: one group enters the wrong gate and takes the wrong way; the other finds the right gate and the sure way. There are two ultimate destinations for people: separation from God forever or living in his home forever. One destination is called "destruction." The other is called "life."

Life is an accurate, broadly descriptive word for heaven. There, as we have seen in this book, life is lived at its fullest and best. Speaking to one of his closest friends who needed encouragement about heaven and the life lived there, Jesus lovingly said, "I am the resurrection and the life. He who believes in me will live, even though he dies; and whoever lives and believes in me will never die. Do you believe this?" (John 11:25-26). Martha needed this clear guidance about entering heaven. Everybody does.

On another occasion Jesus had a personal, serious talk about heaven. This time it was with a highly respected and thoroughly educated Jewish leader—Nicodemus. The essence of this conversation is recorded for us in John 3:1-13. In the stillness of the night hours they lingered long over the subject of the kingdom that would culminate in heaven and the Messiah's eternal reign. At the core of Jesus' teaching on the subject are these words, "Unless a man is born again, he cannot see the kingdom of God" (v. 3). And again, "Unless a man is born of water and the Spirit, he cannot enter the kingdom of God" (v. 5).

This is very clear. A person cannot enter heaven without being born again. Not even a person like Nicodemus has sufficient spiritual strength or merit to enter heaven without being born again. It is a must, an irreducible requirement for every human being on the face of the earth. There is no way around this necessity by using religion or by any other means.

We hear much these days about being born again. The term that Jesus used described a single, specific, spiritual act, but this term is now broadly applied in many areas. There are "born again" athletes who are having a better season this year than last. "Born again" families have gotten back together after separation. "Born again" politicians have gotten excited about politics after a dormant time. This loose usage of "born again" may have weakened our understanding of its original significance. But understanding what Jesus meant is crucial when one realizes that being born again is a requirement for heaven.

By "born again" Jesus spoke of a spiritual experience. It is being born in a radically new fashion. Though not a physical birth, it is something like it because it describes a person who is made new spiritually and is placed in a new family—the family of God. By the new birth the person becomes God's child. An entirely new world—a whole new set of relationships—is opened to the one who is born again. This entire transaction is by the power of God. As a person places faith in Christ as Savior, the power of God is turned in his direction. That person's sins are taken away. Every ounce of guilt is removed. A fresh, divine life is given. This believer is made a new, spiritual creation: he is born again! He now is qualified to enter heaven. The door to his Father's house is opened wide.

Jesus is the only entrance to this experience.

In John 10:9, Jesus states, "I am the gate; whoever enters through me will be saved." And again Jesus declared, "I am the way and the truth and the life. No one comes to the Father except through me" (John 14:6). Some people may think this sounds too exclusive. But the truth is that Jesus is the unique Son of God. After years of observing Christ and listening to him, Peter was convinced that this is the case, so he preached: "Salvation is found in no one else, for there is no other name under heaven given to men by which we must be saved" (Acts 4:12). Peter went on to give his life for this unchangeable truth: Jesus Christ is the only route to eternal life in heaven.

God loves us, and because he loves us he sent Jesus Christ to the world to show us his salvation. Now God is actively involved in attracting people to eternal life. As Paul wrote, God "calls you into his kingdom and glory" (1 Thess. 2:12). This is his continuous, gracious activity. God wants us to choose life, not death. "He called you to this through our gospel, that you might share in the glory of our Lord Jesus Christ" (2 Thess. 2:14). The instrument by which our loving heavenly Father calls people to heaven is the good news of Jesus' death and resurrection for the whole world, because we are all sinners. Each of us can trust Christ personally, be forgiven of our sin, and be assured of entering heaven.

When Peter came to write about the re- lationship of a person to God, he urged all people to make sure of one thing in life—that they possess faith in Jesus the Savior. "Be all the more eager to make your calling and election sure. For if you do these things, you will never fall, and you will receive a rich welcome into the eternal kingdom of our Lord and Savior Jesus Christ" (2 Pet. 1:10-11). This warm and open-hearted apostle exhorts each individual to examine his or her spiritual foundations. He urges them to make their moorings secure in Jesus Christ. God's heaven is precious. Entering into it is at stake.

The Bible closes with a cordial invitation to the human family on earth to come to heaven. This is just what we would expect, because it is the reason for the whole volume of God's Word. " 'Come!' Whoever is thirsty, let him come; and whoever wishes, let him take the free gift of the water of life" (Rev. 22:17). Here, clearly exposed, is the heart of the heavenly Father. He longs for men and women, whoever they are, to come to heaven, his home, using the means he has provided, Jesus Christ his

Son. Only you can exclude yourself from heaven. God doesn't do it. God has made every provision for heaven. But one thing he will never do is violate your will. It is your choice to enter heaven or to stay outside. Everything boils down to a personal decision.

SEVEN
Meet Yourself

Now we close Rita's little card file. You've learned a little about her and perhaps a great deal more about heaven. But the story doesn't end here. It continues with you. Face yourself squarely. Ask yourself whether or not you are on your way to heaven. God has allowed this book to fall into your hands so that you might make this eternal evaluation.

A Christian woman tells of sharing a hospital room with a desperately ill patient. In the middle of the night when only the faint glow of the light at the nurses' station touched the room she heard the lady say, "Where does the soul go when a person dies?" A few minutes later the same question penetrated the room.

Then a third time it came: "Where does the soul go when a person dies?"

The Christian roommate determined that when morning came she would help the lady answer that question by telling her of Jesus the Savior who opens heaven's doors. Then the Christian woman fell asleep. She awoke early the next morning and turned toward the bed from which the question had come those three times in the night. But the bed was empty. The searching woman had died without knowing the answer to life's most crucial question. What remorse for both those ladies!

But you are fortunate. You can ask this burning question, "Where does the soul go when a person dies?" And you can act now upon the answer. This book has been an attempt to help you. Test yourself! Make sure you're headed for heaven.